Spotlight on Equine Nutrition Teleseminar Series

Whole Foods
& Alternative Feeds

Juliet M. Getty, Ph.D.

© 2013 Juliet M. Getty, Ph.D.
All Rights Reserved.

No part of this publication may be reproduced, stored in a retrieval system, or transmitted, in any form or by any means, electronic, mechanical, photocopying, recording or otherwise, without the written permission of the author.

Whole Foods was transcribed from a teleseminar presented by Dr. Juliet M. Getty. Transcription by Darlene J. Backer, CMT (DarleneJBacker@gmail.com). Book design, editing and publication preparation by Elizabeth Testa, Testa Creative Associates (www.TestaCreativeAssociates.com).

ISBN-13: 978-1483969992
ISBN-10: 1483969991

Printed in the United States of America

Preface & Disclaimer

Spotlight on Equine Nutrition: Whole Foods and Alternative Feeds is the transcript of a teleseminar given by Dr. Juliet M. Getty in 2012. This booklet is part of the "Spotlight on Equine Nutrition" series based on Dr. Getty's teleseminars. The goals of offering the transcript in written form are, first, to make it a useful reference resource for anyone to use, and second, to refresh the teleseminar participant's memory of materials covered. It is not necessary for the reader to have attended the teleseminar to get full value from the book.

At all times, Dr. Getty makes every effort to present the most accurate and helpful information based on her expertise and on the most reliable sources. She, her editor, transcriptionist and publisher take no responsibility for any results or damages that might be obtained from the reliance on the information and recommendations made in this book. We further take no responsibility for the inherent risks of activities involving horses, including equine behavior changes that might result in personal injury.

Advice about nutrition, especially in the case of illness, injury, disorders, or conditions requiring medical treatment, is not intended to take the place of proper veterinary care. It may be used in conjunction with such care to facilitate healing and maintain health. The information provided by Getty Equine Nutrition, LLC is presented for the purpose of educating horse owners. Suggested feeds, supplements, and procedures are administered voluntarily with the understanding that any adverse reaction is the responsibility of the owner. Furthermore, Getty Equine Nutrition, LLC cannot be held accountable for a horse's response, whether favorable or adverse, to nutritional intervention.

This is not a verbatim transcript. Obvious comments about technical matters relevant to the teleseminar process have been omitted, along with questions and answers off the specific topic at hand. Some text editing has been done to increase reading ease and text searchability. Mention of a specific product or brand name is not intended to imply that other companies offer inferior products. Dr. Getty means no intention of trademark infringement by the omission of the ® or ™ designation; all product names mentioned are presumed trade-protected.

Juliet M. Getty, Ph.D. is an internationally respected writer and lecturer on equine nutrition. She is the Contributing Nutrition Editor for the *Horse Journal,* and her comprehensive reference book, **Feed Your Horse Like a Horse**, has educated countless horsemen and women in the science behind sound equine feeding practices. She hosts a monthly teleseminar series, one episode of which forms the basis for this adapted transcription. Her informative e-newsletter, *Forage for Thought*, is read by several thousand subscribers every month; she is also available for private consultations and speaking engagements.

The *Spotlight on Equine Nutrition Series* currently offers these teleseminar transcriptions (with more on the way):

Aging Horse
Deciphering Ingredients Lists
Easy Keeper
Feeding for Healthy Joints
Laminitis
Whole Foods

Dr. Getty offers a generous serving of other equine nutrition knowledge at www.GettyEquineNutrition.com.

Whole Foods
& Alternative Feeds

Introduction

As we begin talking about this topic of introducing some different kinds of feeds into your horse's diet, we know that our common goal is for you to have a healthy horse. A healthy horse just looks healthy, doesn't he? His eyes are bright, his movements are supple, his hair coat is thick and shiny and healthy, his hooves are hard and free of cracks, and he has no infections. His respiration is smooth and his disposition is calm—the way you want your horse to be, receptive to you and not overly sensitive.

The way you get your horse to be healthy is to feed him correctly, and that includes him giving all of the nutrients that he needs. That's where whole foods come into the picture, because they can help us do that.

Chapter One
Defining "Whole" and Other Terminology

Before we get into specifics, let me define what "whole" means. There are two ways to think about it. One way is to think of a whole food, perhaps a whole grain like whole wheat, for example. The whole wheat kernel is a substance that contains a variety of parts. The outer hull is called the bran. You're probably familiar with wheat bran. We sometimes feed this to horses; it's high in fiber. Then there is the starchy center called the endosperm—we make white flour out of that. We don't normally feed wheat flour of any kind to horses but we do sometimes feed oat flour. And then there is the part I like to call the powerhouse of the wheat kernel, or any kind of seed, and that's called the germ. The germ is where the nutrients are really concentrated; it contains fat and protein and carbohydrates and vitamins and minerals. The germ feeds the plant's first sprouting—it allows the plant to germinate, hence the name "germ." So the whole grain then contains all of these parts: the bran, the endosperm, and the germ. They are the parts of the whole; each has valuable benefits to contribute. We can feed all of these things separately or we can feed them as the whole grain.

The second way of defining a whole food is to think of it as one that is unadulterated or in its natural state; in other words, it has nothing added. There are no preservatives or fillers in it, so it's whole in the sense that it is in the state nature intended.

The foundation of a horse's diet should be a particular whole food, and that is grass—all day and all night, all the time. The horse needs to have forage, grass, flowing through his digestive tract all the time with no gaps, because that's the way the horse's digestive system is designed. This is for several reasons. First, his stomach produces acid all the time, regardless of whether it has food to process, and continuous feeding protects against ulcerative damage from that constant supply of acid. Processing forage also helps to keep the muscles of the digestive tract moving and toned up to process nutrients and ward off colic. A horse with an empty stomach can suffer a variety of disorders, not only ulcers and colic, but also laminitis, diarrhea, insulin resistance, and more. For more on this, see Appendix A: Feeding Free Choice, at the back of this book.

Grass, then, is the most important whole food. Grass can be a perfect food, as well, especially if it's from a healthy "whole food" pasture that contains a variety of forages, rather than an "improved" pasture of, for example, all timothy or all orchard grass.

Notice I did not say hay. That is because when you take grass and you cut it and you dry it and you store it, it loses a lot of things. In fact, hay is nutritionally dismal. Yes, it contains protein and it contains fiber, both of which are important. It can contain a little bit of fat, too, but most of the vitamins are gone. And even though many of the minerals are still there, hay is such an incomplete food that we really need to supplement it in some fashion. Start by getting it analyzed so you know where to go from there.

Let's talk about why I emphasize variety in pasture grasses. In a wild setting, horses will not limit themselves to eating grasses. They eat flowers and leaves and cereal grains and nuts and herbs and all kinds of plants; they achieve balance in their diet naturally. In a domestic situation, we want to mimic this by striving to provide variety.

Before we talk about specific foods to add, let's talk about vitamins and minerals. Yes, these particular nutrients are best supplied by giving a variety of foods like fruits and vegetables and herbs and flowers and teas and so on, but there are three very important points to understand here.

- **First:** Hay is so devoid of many nutrients that it is really difficult to adequately supplement by simply adding some fruits and vegetables. Consider how much grass your horse eats when he is on pasture. If you assume around a 50% water level in the forage, he would probably eat somewhere around 35 or 40 pounds of grass. There is likely no way that you could feed the equivalent 35-40 pounds of carrots and apples or any other fruits and vegetables. That is why, when you're feeding all or even mostly hay, you need to provide a vitamin/mineral supplement to fill in the gaps. However, we can still add fruits and vegetables to reduce the amount of supplementation, and also to provide trace nutrients that aren't typically found in supplements.

- **Second:** I want you also to understand the difference between a *pharmacological* dose of nutrients and a *physiological* dose of nutrients. Think of an orange, for example. A small orange has about 60 mg of vitamin C. That amount of vitamin C is a little more than the amount we humans would need to prevent scurvy; it's the baseline amount we need to maintain basic health. But let's say you are suffering from some immune system disorder, maybe you have allergies or you're suffering from an infection or maybe you have inflammation in your body or you just need more antioxidant help, then taking more vitamin C would help treat whatever's ailing you. So the *physiological* dose from the orange would be the 60 mg but a *pharmacological* dose would be far more than that—you might take 500 mg or 1000 mg of vitamin C to help treat your ailment.

  The same is true for horses. If a horse is doing fine at a maintenance level, then we need to just make sure he gets a basic (*physiological*) amount, which fresh grass in a healthy pasture will usually provide, but if he has any kind of disorder or condition that warrants additional nutrients, then we need to give these nutrients at *pharmacological* levels.

- **Third:** Adding new foods to the diet must be done carefully. The hindgut bacteria population needs to be introduced to something new on a gradual basis to allow it to adapt. Then any food given in quantity should be given consistently. For example, warm bran mash can be a comfort food for a horse on a cold, wintry night, but offering it only once a week is very dangerous because the hindgut bacteria can't shift gears that quickly. I have known this to lead to colic in more than one instance, so I want to impress upon you that if you want to feed bran, whether it be warm or not, you have to do it every day. Variety in the diet must be introduced gradually and tempered with consistency.

Keep in mind that whole foods can vary in their nutritional values. Just because you have an apple or an orange or a banana doesn't necessarily mean that it has everything in it that it's supposed to have. It might have been grown in depleted soil, for example, or it might have been harvested too soon or stored improperly or exposed to water or sunlight damage—any number of issues can affect the nutritional value of that fruit or vegetable. For this discussion, though, we need to make some assumptions, so we're going to assume that the foods we're discussing are at least somewhat nutritious.

One other wrinkle: Understand that vitamins are very sensitive. They can be destroyed by oxygen, they can be destroyed by heat, by light, by moisture. If you take an orange, for example, and cut it in half and leave it sitting on your kitchen counter for an hour, when you come back half of the vitamin C that was in that orange will be gone because vitamin C is an antioxidant and oxygen will destroy it. This is even true if you have orange juice in a container; as soon as you open up the container and let oxygen in, then the vitamin C starts to deteriorate. Vitamin C supplements for your horses are equally vulnerable. Every time you open up the container and let oxygen in, you destroy some of the vitamin C. So, remember, when buying vitamins, you want to buy a quantity that will last no longer than six months so that they stay the freshest. And keep them in a cool, dry place with the lid tightly closed between uses.

Minerals, on the other hand, are indestructible; you cannot destroy a mineral. They can be solubilized—if the hay gets wet—for example, if you soak your hay to remove sugar and starch for your insulin resistant horse—then you're also removing a lot of minerals. So minerals can be lost, but they'll never be destroyed.

Sometimes when we talk about minerals, we differentiate between whether they are in an inorganic form or in the organically chelated form. The way minerals exist in fruits and vegetables is *inorganic* but inside the horse's digestive tract, it's a different story. The horse's digestion has the capability of *chelating* (attaching) the mineral to an amino acid which facilitates the absorption of that mineral into the bloodstream. However, this type of chelation is not very efficient and so absorption of minerals is not very high, so providing a product with a chelated version of a mineral will help improve the bioavailability (or absorption) of that mineral.

Let's get into specifics.

Chapter Two
Food Lists

Chapter 10 in my book, ***Feed Your Horse Like a Horse,*** covers a lot about which foods to feed and which to avoid. But most of what we're covering tonight is not in my book, and I strive to do that with all of these teleseminars.

Foods to Avoid

First let's talk about things to avoid. You want to avoid anything that belongs to the nightshade family. This would be tomatoes or peppers (sweet peppers or hot peppers) and raw white potatoes (cooked are okay). Also, I think it's good to avoid feeding cruciferous vegetables such as broccoli, cabbage, cauliflower, kale, and Brussels sprouts; they're not really toxic but they can produce excessive amounts of gas which can bring on a gas colic. I've heard of people giving a small amount of broccoli but I would not feed it in any kind of quantity.

Avoid things that are high in sugar. I wouldn't feed sugar cubes or peppermints. Oh, I suppose if you give your horse a peppermint once in a while, it's not going to harm him, but it's certainly not contributing to his health. If you're going to feed him something extra, make it count nutritionally.

And now, the good stuff, not in any particular order.

Some general notes to start:

1. Remember, whenever you're feeding fruits and vegetables, it's good to cut them up into pieces that are longer than they are wide. The horse can chew them better, so they don't get stuck in the back teeth.

2. Some people will soak the fruit or vegetable, especially if they're going to feed the skins, in a diluted vinegar solution overnight. This has the advantage of removing any pesticides, bacteria or fungicidal residues that are on the outside of the skin. I don't see any problem with this.

3. Some caution is in order when feeding fruit to the insulin resistant horse. In the Library section of my website (www.gettyequinenutrition.com) there is an article entitled "Fruits for the Insulin-Resistant Horse." In it, I list a lot of different fruits and their grams of sugars and how fruit can be safely incorporated into the diet for an insulin-resistant horse.

Edible Incredible Treats

Beets, and the greens of beets, are wonderful. Bananas, oh my, horses love bananas, and you don't even have to peel them. In fact, banana peels are a good low-sugar way to add the taste of banana to your horse's diet if he's insulin resistant and can't eat the actual fruit (the banana itself is pretty high in sugar). Celery, sweet potatoes, squash and pumpkin. Lettuce, even dark leafy lettuce, if your horse will eat it. Those old standbys, carrots and apples. Plantains, green beans, these are all wonderful. Unshelled peas are also very nice.

Dates are good, but remove the pit. I had a client who had a date tree and her horse loved it, too much, I might say; we had to remove that from his diet to some extent because he was overweight and at risk of experiencing laminitis. Raisins and grapes are also beneficial. Then there are the berries; every kind of berry—blueberries, raspberries, boysenberries, blackberries, strawberries—is excellent. Tropical fruits like mango and papaya, but make sure you remove the pit. Cranberries, cherries, but again, remove the pit. Citrus fruits like oranges, orange rinds and lemon rinds, grapefruits rinds, these are nice. I have yet to see a horse that doesn't like watermelon—very cooling and a source of water. The watermelon rinds can be cut up into small pieces and offered as a low sugar treat. Pomegranates can be cut up, peel and all, and pureed in a blender for a very sweet treat.

Sunflowers seeds (but see my caution later about omega 6s), pumpkin seeds, certainly flax seeds (although they should be ground because they're so small). Peanuts are also good but they should be roasted to kill the aflatoxins (a type of mycotoxin) they naturally contain—no salt added, please, since you are likely offering salt from another source.

Don't forget herbs and flowers. Rose hips are very high in vitamin C. Parsley and marigolds are also very tasty for horses. And you can even feed freeze-dried fruits and herbs, which are more nutritious than most processed foods.

Have you ever made tea for your horse? Last summer, when I went out to visit my recently arrived horses, I had a glass of iced tea in my hand, and my horse started to drink it. After that happened a couple of times, I made up a big bowl of iced tea for him and his companion, and they just loved it. Avoid anything that's caffeinated, though; I don't think caffeine is a good idea for horses. But peppermint tea, chamomile tea, any kind of herbal tea would be wonderful for horses. I noticed the chamomile tea did make my horses a little sleepy.

Sometimes give Skode's treats; maybe you're familiar with those. They're wonderful.

That's not a complete list by any means, but it covers a lot. When in doubt you can look it up (Google it!) or you can contact me and I'll be happy to help you. There are so many different things to choose from for the occasional treat.

Chapter Three
About Protein and Its Sources

What about whole food protein sources? One of the things your hay analysis[i] tells you is the amount of crude protein; however, the crude protein percentage doesn't tell you anything about the quality of the protein. Protein quality has to do with the amino acid balance. All protein sources contain all of the *essential* amino acids, of which there are ten. (Essential means that the body can't produce it, yet it's necessary for the diet. There are twelve more amino acids that the body can make.) However, these essential amino acids are not always in the proper proportion to each other, and that disproportion reduces the quality of the protein. If some essential amino acids are present in lesser amounts, the body's ability to synthesize proteins (e.g., muscle, hooves, hair, blood proteins, antibodies, etc.) is limited. The extra amino acids get destroyed—the horse cannot store them to use to balance protein later.

That's why you have to make sure your are feeding a good quality protein. The best way to do that is to mix your sources to include foods that add the amino acids that are in short supply in their forage, thereby raising the quality of the protein and making it more available to the body (or "complete"). This will ensure there are enough amino acids to build body proteins and to build tissue throughout the body.

You see, when the horse's hair and hooves and skin suffer, it tells you that he's not getting enough nutrients to feed those organs and tissues, because the horse uses what he has in order of priority. It shouldn't come as a surprise that his priority is to keep his lungs breathing and his heart beating and his liver functioning, so those organs are going to get first dibs on what's available. Only if there are amino acids left over will the hooves and the joints and the

---

i. Take samples from the inside of several bales, even up to 20. If you have a probe, that's great; if you don't, then just take it along the length of the bale on the inside and from several bales. Send in a sample to a lab. Equi-Analytical (www.equi-analytical.com) is a good choice because they are an equine-specific lab.

hair coat be fed. These are secondary tissues that are not necessary for life, so when they're healthy, it tells you that the rest of the horse's body is getting adequate nutrition for health.

Certainly you want to have forage as the foundation. It's very good news that protein doesn't change much from grass to hay. (In fact, you'd have to put the hay in some very, very rough environmental conditions for the protein to be destroyed.) But you can also feed forage as a carrier to add other whole foods or supplements if you need to boost protein. Hay pellets are a very nice way to do that. You can buy timothy, orchard grass, and alfalfa pellets. Choose a product that doesn't have any added preservatives or additives. (I've even seen hay pellets with animal fat added—not a good thing.) Pellets can be moistened, which I prefer, to prevent any kind of choking issue. Moistened pellets make a really nice base for adding all kinds of things. Standlee makes quality hay products.

Beet pulp Beet pulp contains some protein (approximately 7%) and offers more amino acid variety to your horse's diet. Check with the provider to see if it's genetically modified, if that's a concern to you, or if it has pesticides added. It's hard to find, but organic beet pulp does exist. If the horse needs to gain weight, beet pulp doesn't have a high NSC level and so it is a nice way to add calories without the risk of raising the blood insulin levels. NSC in beet pulp can be as low as 4% or as high as 19, but generally on average it's around 10 or 12%, which is a very nice level. **Alfalfa pellets**, to compare, have an NSC level of around 10%, which is also good, whereas a grass hay pellet like a timothy pellet can have an NSC level of around 14%, verging on unacceptable for the insulin resistant horse.

Soybean hulls are also a good source of mixing protein, with a very low NSC at around 4-5%. They are very high in digestible fiber, and don't let the fact that this is a byproduct scare you--byproduct simply means that it's part of the whole. The hull is the part that's concentrated in fiber. Soybean hulls are often added to commercial feeds; however, they can be hard to find on their own.

Those are some of the more traditional types of protein sources. Some other, less usual, sources are out there, too.

Copra is basically coconut meal after most of the fat has been taken out. It has about 20% protein so it's a high protein source. It's also very high in fiber. (It does contain a considerable amount of fat, and I'll talk about it again when I talk about fat sources.) Copra is not a complete protein; you have to mix it with something else to get the balanced amino acids that create a high quality protein. Depending on the size of the horse, I wouldn't feed more than 1.5-2 pounds of copra per day, but it is something worth considering. You want to make sure to buy it from a source that monitors their mycotoxin levels because copra can harbor mycotoxins. So be sure to choose a reliable source–CoolStance is a good product for that; it's made by Stance Equine (www.stanceequine.co.uk).

Soy is also a wonderful protein source. It's 45% protein; in fact, soybeans have the highest quality of protein among all plants. If you're a vegetarian, then you know the benefits of eating soy. The protein quality in soy is so high that you really don't need to rely on mixing it with anything else. (It's almost as high in quality as fish or eggs.) Fermented soy would be better for horses, but I don't think you can find fermented soy products like miso or tempeh in any kind of quantity. At the very least, though, make sure that it is heat treated to inactivate a substance known as a trypsin inhibitor that interferes with protein digestion. By the way, most soy products come from genetically modified plants.

Note, also, that many horses are sensitive to soy; they get gas from it or they may actually be allergic to it. Sometimes they may exhibit unusual behavior, such as stallion-like demonstrations in geldings. The reason is still unidentified, but I think it may be because soy (also alfalfa, to a lesser extent) contains plant forms of estrogen known as phytoestrogens which may affect behavior. Some horses develop laminitis because of soy; again we don't have the facts but I think the phytoestrogens may play somewhat of a role in that as well.

Hemp seeds contain a little less protein than soy (36%) but are comparable in their protein quality. They contain albumin, a very high quality protein that is found in egg whites And unlike soy, they do not contain a trypsin inhibitor, so they can be fed raw. Furthermore, they do not contain high amounts of phytoestrogens. Finally, they are less gas-producing than soy. As you'll read later, they are high in fat, especially omega 6s, and therefore should be balanced with omega 3s.

Flaxseed meal and **chia see**ds are also excellent sources of protein. We think of them in terms of fat but they are also good sources of protein and fiber. Chia seeds contain more mucilages or water-soluble fibers than flax does, so that's why they form more of a gel. But for either of these, normally feed no more than a pound a day. Omega 3s are very important but to keep them in balance you don't want to overdo them.

Sunflower seed meal is very high in protein. It does contain a lot of omega-6 fatty acids, which we'll discuss further one, but it might be worthwhile for adding protein.

Pumpkin seeds are excellent sources of protein.

Peanuts (not really a nut, but a legume) are good but remember, they should be roasted to eliminate aflatoxins.

Lentils are also great at about 20% protein.

Split peas—very tasty to horses— are a wonderful way to boost the overall quality of the protein. I buy mine from the Bulk Foods website.

Alfalfa, of course, is also a legume; a nice way to improve protein quality is to mix grass hay with some alfalfa. Alfalfa also has the wonderful benefit of being a natural buffering agent. This is especially helpful for horses that are prone to developing ulcers. However, I would never feed more than 50% of the hay ration as alfalfa.

There another protein sources you might not be aware of. This is **whey**; this is about 20-30% crude protein and is very tasty to a horse. You can get it at Bulk Foods. Honeyville Grain and Platinum Performance also carry it.

So… little bits of hemp and whey and split peas and almond flour and flaxseed meal and pumpkin seeds…you get the picture? A little bit of this and a little bit of that, and you end up having a horse that has all the amino acids at his disposal to make every protein that he needs.

Chapter Four
Foods for Certain Health Problems

Certain whole foods can be particularly helpful for specific health conditions.

Joints and hoof health

Joints and hoof health rely on collagen production; vitamin C is necessary for the production of collagen, so foods that are high in vitamin C, like citrus fruits, rose hips, and berries, are wonderful for collagen production. Another important substance that's needed for collagen production is the amino acid proline; chia seeds, which we'll talk more about later, are particularly high in proline.

Digestion

Many horses suffer digestion problems, maybe an ulcer or diarrhea, or a lot of gas formation, and chia seeds again are a good choice because chia seeds are particularly high in mucilages. Mucilages are water-soluble fibers that form a soothing gel in the digestive tract. Another digestive aid would be brewer's yeast. Brewer's yeast (saccharomyces cerevisiae) is the yeast that's often added to different feeds, and it is very helpful in healing the digestive tract.

Here's a nutrient extracted from plant cells (mainly soy) that you may not be familiar with: lecithin. Here's why you will want know about it: The stomach and digestive tract lining (the epithelium) can be damaged by naturally occurring stomach acid or the use of nonsteroidal anti-inflammatory drugs (i.e. Bute, Banamine, even Equioxx). This can lead to digestive problems and lecithin helps with that. Lecithin is a type of phospholipid that helps the digestive tract heal by restoring the epithelium. The most common version of lecithin on the market is phosphatidylcholine.

To understand lecithin's role, first you have to understand how nonsteroidal anti-inflammatory drugs (NSAIDs) reduce pain and inflammation. We tend to assume that it is the NSAID itself that is directly irritating the stomach lining.

In actuality, the damage happens after the NSAID has been absorbed. NSAIDs such as bute inhibit the cyclooxygenase enzymes 1 and 2; these enzymes reduce the formation of prostaglandins which promote inflammation and pain but they can also reduce the prostaglandins that maintain the integrity of the entire digestive tract by stimulating the production of phospholipids. Phospholipids (lecithin) form a barrier to help prevent stomach acid from damaging the underlying epithelium.

You can see why I say lecithin is a wonderful thing to feed. I usually suggest feeding about a half cup a day. You can buy lecithin and other spices and flours in bulk online; I buy mine at Bulk Foods (www.bulkfoods.com). It also has a lot of chocolate, which is nice for me, not for my horses though (laughter on recording).

Insulin Resistance

Insulin resistance is another condition that affects many horses, and omega-3 fatty acids have been shown to help by increasing insulin sensitivity (receptiveness) or, in other words, decreasing insulin resistance. Omega 3s are found in appreciable quantity in flaxseed meal and chia seeds. They're also found in fish oils, which I'll talk about later on. You can learn more about the insulin resistant horse in two other teleseminars, *Laminitis* and *The Easy Keeper*; these are available as audio recordings and in print through my website.

Allergies and Immune Responses

Allergies can be helped with nettles, an herb; quercetin, which is a type of bioflavonoid (considered to have antioxidant, anti-inflammatory properties); and rose hips. Rose hips are high in vitamin C but they also contain lycopenes, which are a type of bioflavonoid. Bioflavonoids are largely found in the pulp of fruits such as oranges, pomegranates and watermelon. (They are, for the record, also found in tomatoes which I absolutely wouldn't give to your horses!) Almond skins also contain bioflavonoids, so sliced almonds are also wonderful for horses that have any kind of allergies. Other types of immune responses benefit from B vitamins and aloe vera (if it comes from the leaf). This is interesting to note if your horse suffers from any kind of immune problem: The pulpy leaf of the aloe vera plant contains an immunostimulant that's called acemannan.

Lethargy

If your horse seems lethargic, take a look at the B vitamins. There are eight B vitamins, all working in concert with one another. The hindgut microbial population can product all eight; however anything that compromises their numbers (e.g., mental stress, pain, infection, antibiotics, large amounts of starchy feeds, forage restriction) increases the need for dietary sources. Foods that provide B vitamins include almonds, peanuts, seeds, wheat germ, and brewer's yeast.

Inflammation

Inflammation is another common problem that presents itself in horses in a variety of ways: laminitis, tendon or ligament injuries, joint and muscle strain. Lots of things help with this.

Anthocyanidins, which are COX-2 inhibitors (anti-inflammatories), are found in rose hips and almonds. All the **berries**, especially blueberries, are very high in them, and also **pomegranates**. **Curcumin**, the active ingredient in the spice, turmeric, is a potent anti-inflammatory. One of my horses has an old racing injury that presented as a very swollen fetlock when I first got him; I've been giving him two tablespoons of turmeric a day—it's really making a significant difference in the way that he feels. Start with small amounts because it does have a strong taste. (I am also giving him lecithin.)

Another very potent anti-inflammatory agent is the **amino acid arginine**. Arginine increases nitric oxide which improves circulation. Whenever you improve circulation you bring more blood to the injured or inflamed area, which helps remove free radicals (especially if there are antioxidants available to the body) and also helps with healing. (For more, see Appendix B: Antioxidants, the Unsung Heroes.) This is particularly important for tendon and ligament injuries as well as laminitis. You can buy the commercial supplement, arginine alpha ketoglutarate (abbreviated AAKG). Or you can give foods that are high in arginine—**wheat germ, oranges, brewer's yeast, chia** and **flax seeds, pumpkin** and other forms of **squash**.

Sliced **almonds** are wonderful, but be careful of feeding whole almonds, which the horse may not chew adequately; you can also add almond flour to your horse's feed. Honeyville Food Products (www.HoneyvilleGrain.com) sells almond flour and other foods in bulk as well.

Flaxseed meal and chia seeds are helpful for inflammation, too because of their high omega 3 content.

Another effective means of combating inflammation is **colloidal silver** because it has antimicrobial properties. It's sometimes hard to find for horses; Dr. Mark DePaolo (DVM) offers colloidal silver on his website, www.DePaoloEquineConcepts.com.

Chapter Five
A Few Words About Fats

There are different types of fat. In general categories, these are saturated fat, monounsaturated fat, and polyunsaturated fat (which includes the omega 3s and omega 6s). Omega 9s are monounsaturated. Let me refer you here to another article in the Library section on my website, www.gettyequinenutrition.com, for an article on omegas entitled "Fat is Fat, Right? No - Check Your Omegas!" It will help sort out these different omega types of fatty acids. In *Feed Your Horse Like a Horse*, there's a chart on page 47 on common fat sources and what they contain.

Coconut oil. Remember the copra meal made from coconuts? Stance Equine also offers a product called PowerStance, which is the ***coconut oil***. The copra meal is a good source of protein, and it contains about 8% fat, but, of course, the coconut oil is 100% fat. People ask me about coconut oil all the time. You'll find claims about the stability of coconut oil, how it's great to feed because it won't easily go rancid, but that to me is not a reason to feed it. The reason that it's stable is because the fatty acids in coconut oil (for the most part—not all of them) are saturated. Chemically, a saturated fatty acid has no double bonds; a double bond creates a vulnerable spot in the carbon chain of a fatty acid where oxygen can damage it (cause it to go rancid). So a saturated fatty acid cannot go rancid. That sounds like a good thing, but the problem is that horses are not accustomed to having large amounts of saturated fat in their diet. Horses are plant eaters; they are herbivorous. Saturated fat for the most part is found in animal fat. Coconut oil, of course, is plant-based but it does contain saturated fat. Furthermore, we don't have any studies to show its effect long term on the blood vessels and the heart of the horse. I am uncomfortable feeding coconut oil in most instances.

Notice that I say *in most instances*, but I don't say *always*. There are different forms of saturated fat. The fat in coconut oil is called a medium-chained fatty acid. Studies have shown that medium-chain fatty acids do have antiviral, antifungal, and antibacterial properties and therefore they may have a beneficial medicinal application. If you have a horse suffering from any kind of immune problem or exposed to large amounts of viruses or bacteria (such as from distant travels or exposure to new environs or horses), then I think adding some coconut oil in small amounts would be a useful short-term approach.

Rice bran. Another source of fat is rice bran. It has about 25% NSC so if you have an insulin resistant horse, go easy on this. The fat in rice bran, however, is very safe for helping an underweight horse gain some weight because it is mostly in the monounsaturated form. Monounsaturates do not promote inflammation nor do they decrease it; they are inert. They may be beneficial for the heart, although the studies done to date have been on humans, not horses. Rice bran has about 10 times more phosphorus than calcium, so you need to correct that ratio. You can use a stabilized product that has a little bit of extra calcium added, or you can feed something that's high in calcium such as alfalfa or beet pulp to balance it out.

Peanut oil is high in monounsaturates, as is **olive oil**. I know a few people who feed olive oil but it's not very popular. Many horses don't care for it; it has a rather strong taste.

Omega fatty acids

This brings me to a discussion of omega 6s. Omega 6s are important—in particular, the one that's called linoleic acid. This is considered an essential fatty acid because the horse's body cannot make it so therefore it must be provided in the diet. The problem with omega 6s occurs when we have too much in relationship to omega 3s. This is very common in commercially fortified horse feeds with added soybean oil, which has about 50% omega 6s. When you add an oil that's high in omega 6s, you increase the propensity toward inflammation. If the horse is already somewhat inflamed—maybe because he's working or performing or in training, or he's older and has arthritis—then you aggravate that inflammation. So I recommend balancing out the omega 6s by offering fat sources that are high in omega 3s. Fresh grass has four times more omega 3s than omega 6s. That is the naturally occurring ratio that we're striving to equal, a 4:1 omega 3:omega 6 ratio.

The wonderful **ground flaxseed meal** is an excellent way of adding omega 3s in the proper ratio. But note: Don't feed flax seeds whole and don't boil them or soak them, please, because that makes the fatty acids start to go rancid. Their shelf life is short anyway, so if you opt to grind them yourself, you will want to do it on a daily basis. **Chia seeds** are also excellent for this. Chia seeds are more stable, and you don't have to grind them.

Sunflower seeds are a common addition to the diet. They're high in quality proteins but the oil in sunflower seeds is very high at 71% omega 6s; only safflower seeds exceed this, but sunflower seeds run a close second.

And then there are the **fish oils**. Fish oils I do not usually recommend simply because horses don't eat fish. Fish oils have a different kind of omega 3s. The omega 3s that are found in chia and flax consist of an essential fatty acid known as alpha linolenic acid or ALA. The omega 3s found in fish oils are not essential; they are docosahexaenoic acid (DHA) or eicosapentaenoic acid (EPA), and supplementing these can be helpful for horses that have extreme levels of inflammation. That's when I recommend them, but generally speaking I do not add fish oils to a horse's diet.

Hemp seed oil is a good source of omega 3s; however it has more omega 6s. The ratio is about 2.5:1 omega 6:omega 3 so it's a little inverted. The nice thing about hemp oil, however, is that it contains gamma linolenic acid (GLA) which is a type of omega 6, but it doesn't increase inflammation; instead it actually has anti-inflammatory properties. So hemp oil is okay in moderation.

Soybean oil, as I mentioned, is mostly omega 6s. It does contain some omega 3s, about 7%. And by the way, beware of feeds with soybean oil that are advertised as containing omega 3s. Are these claims lying? No, it has omega 3s (7%), but from a concentrated source? Absolutely not. Does it have a high amount of omega 6s? Absolutely. Read your labels carefully.

Wheat germ oil (a good source of vitamin E) is about half omega 6s.

Grapeseed oil is mostly omega 6s, about 70%, so it does have inflammatory properties. **Grapeseed extract**, on the other hand, consists of the antioxidants that exist naturally in grape seeds. Called proanthocyanidins, these are a type of flavonoid and are potent antioxidants and anti-inflammatories.

Three fats to avoid!

Corn oil is mostly omega 6s. It has no omega 3s and little nutritional value, and so it is just not a good choice. Put that low on the list.

Cocosoya oil is a popular feed additive often given to horses to make the meal more palatable. Coconut oil, as I mentioned, should be used more in small quantities as a medicine chest item than as a daily menu item. The "soya" in cocosoya is that soybean oil we've been discussing which is so high in omega 6s. (This is true for you, too, by the way. If you have arthritis or any kind of pain in your body, take a look at how much soybean oil you're eating. It's in many, many products and it's highly inflammatory.)

Cool Calories. The main ingredient in the product called Cool Calories is partially hydrogenated vegetable oil, which is the same as trans fat. Trans fats are a type of processed fat that is so harmful to the human body, the FDA requires it to be listed on food labels. Why in the world would you give something like that to your horses? You can tell if something contains trans fats if the label says it contains any "partially hydrogenated" oil. Even if a human food item label says 0 grams of trans fat, that's per serving. If the label reads partially hydrogenated vegetable oil, and if you eat more than one serving, then you're getting some trans fat. Put it down and find something else. And definitely don't give trans fats in any form, including Cool Calories, to your horse.

Conclusion

You can see from all this that whole foods can be part of a nutritious feeding plan so that your horse's diet is sufficiently varied and well-rounded to ensure his good health. We'll move on now to your questions.

Take samples from the inside of several bales, even up to 20. If you have a probe, that's great; if you don't, then just take it along the length of the bale on the inside and from several bales. Send in a sample to a lab. Equi-Analytical is a good choice because they specialize in equine tests, and so their results provide numbers that are relevant to horses. They are at www.equi-analytical.com.

Chapter Six
Questions & Answers

Fodder Systems. Leslie asks about fodder systems, in particular one from FarmTek, and which products she should grow this way.

> *Answer.* There are many different fodder systems around. Fodder usually just means feed but here what we're talking about is growing grass by hydroponically sprouting various foods like barley or oats or alfalfa or sunflowers, and producing a product that is very nutritious. The systems look very interesting; you can research it at FarmTek's Fodder System site (http://foddersystems.com). What concerns me about these are the nutritional values. First on my mind is the NSC level, the nonstructural carbohydrates, particularly for the horse that cannot tolerate high levels of sugars and starches. In the FarmTek information, some of the product details don't list the sugar and starch content but the barley one does; barley fodder, which is sprouted barley, has a combined 24% of sugars and starch, which is on the very high side. They don't list the sugars/starch content for their sunflower sprouts but the fat is quite high at 29%; if you have an overweight horse you certainly wouldn't want to feed a forage source with almost a third of its calories from fat. Alfalfa fodder is not shown on the website but I would expect that would be the safest one. I would probably mix it with some type of grass so that you don't feed all alfalfa.

Heaves and Hay Analysis. Suzanne in Costa Rica says the local hay suppliers are very limited and it's hard to find good quality hay. She has a mare that suffers from heaves and is susceptible to laminitis. There are no labs in her area that test for NSC, so she wants to know how to vary the diet safely.

> *Answer.* That question is a little broader than I can answer here, Suzanne, but let's take your question in parts. First of all, getting your horse out into fresh air is the first thing that you want to do for heaves; make sure your horse is not stalled and has access to fresh air and not in a dusty en-

vironment. To treat the heaves I recommend vitamin C at between 3 and 10 mg per pound of body weight in a pharmacological dose. C is a natural antioxidant, as I've mentioned, but it's also a natural antihistamine so it lowers the respiratory reaction. Even from Costa Rica, you can send a hay sample to Equi-Analytical Labs (www.equi-analytical.com), so you will know what you have in your forage, and then get a good vitamin/mineral supplement to fill in the gaps. You may need to add some of the protein sources that I mentioned tonight as well as some fruits and vegetables, and flaxseed meal or chia seeds or flaxseed oil would beneficial for omega 3s.

Ration Balancer. Susan has been boarding her horse ever since she's owned him and he gets a small amount of commercial feed to carry his supplements, but now she has an opportunity to move him to a backyard situation. With this change in situation, she can also make changes in his feeding program. She would like to understand whether there are benefits to using a ration balancer instead of grain.

Answer. First, we need to be clear on definitions. To me, a "ration balancer" is another way of saying a vitamin/mineral supplement that you would add to a hay-based diet. I think by "grain" you mean some sort of a commercial complete feed. (In the old days we would think of just adding oats for a supplement. We've really gotten away from considering plain oats the go-to choice.) A complete feed supposedly can be fed without any forage but I don't recommend doing that. Generally the word "complete" means that all the vitamins and minerals are there, but only if you feed it according to directions; you can't just feed it in a small amount as a carrier. Amounts to achieve that "complete" level can vary depending on the manufacturer, some as much as 15 pounds a day, which is obviously not feasible. So I would suggest that you feed a carrier such as some hay and/or alfalfa pellets and then add a vitamin/mineral supplement—there's your ration balancer. I recommend Glanzen Complete (a custom-made preparation available on my website or through Horsetech), which is a flaxseed meal-based preparation that has high amounts of vitamin C and vitamin E to fill in the gaps. There are others; ADM makes something called Grow Strong, Triple Crown has something called 30% Equine Supplement (but it is mostly soy so you might not wish to consider that). Of course, if you can feed some whole foods, too, then you can reduce the amount of supplementation that you need.

Grains, Whole Foods, Laminae Issues. Jane wonders if there has been any definitive research showing a direct correlation between feeding grains and laminitic hoof events. She cites an example of a friend who feeds her young horse grain with molasses, to no apparent ill effect.

Answer. Jane, yes, absolutely there is a proven correlation, for two reasons. There has been much research to substantiate grain's increasing the propensity toward developing osteopathic disorders such as physitis or epiphysitis. So one should never, never, never feed a growing horse a feed that's high in starch. ADM Alliance has a good product called Junior Glow. I think Triple Crown's growth formula is low in starch but Purina Junior, for example, is very high in sugar and starch. So stay away from sweet feeds. That's the first thing. But the second thing really addresses your question: There is a lot of research to explain how starchy sweet feeds increase the risk of laminitis simply because of their glycemic response; in other words, starchy sweet feeds significantly raise blood glucose levels, causing a surge of insulin secretion from the pancreas. Elevated insulin levels increase inflammation in the hoof, leading to the separation of the laminae from the hoof wall. There's lot of research on that.

Salads, Hoof Rings. Jane also asks why some people can seemingly feed their horses all kinds of salads, have no issues and horses that look fantastic, but when she tried it once, rings appeared on her horses' hooves within a month. Is there any connection between pumpkin seeds, yams, greens, etc., and problems with the foot?

Answer. You know, this is a tough one because I don't really know what else you were feeding, but if the horse has a genetic tendency toward insulin resistance, then insulin is already high so when you add more sugar (such as with the yams), even if it's something from a worthwhile nutritious food, it pushes the insulin over the top and can cause laminitis. You really have to be careful and you may not be able to feed large amounts of some fruits and vegetables to your horses if they're insulin resistant.

Spotlight on Equine Nutrition Series

Protein Increase for Insulin Resistant Horse. Deb has an insulin-resistant horse and she wants to increase her protein intake. She currently gives three-quarters of a cup of soaked yellow split peas per day with a little beet pulp, but her horse is a very easy keeper and so she wants to see if there's anything else that she can offer.

Answer. We've already covered quite a few options in the lecture section, so I'll review here. Split peas are wonderful but they are high in starch. Therefore, reduce the amount you feed to ½ cup. Instead of beet pulp, perhaps go with some alfalfa pellets; they're a little lower in sugar and starch than beet pulp. To improve protein quality, the split peas are worthwhile, and you can also add whey or hemp seeds, some almond flour or sliced almonds.

Mixing protein sources is a good way to ensure that the horse is getting enough amino acids to build body proteins. You do want to make sure she has all the grass hay that she wants. She shouldn't run out because the hormonal response to an empty stomach will keep her fat; also, you want to make sure that she gets plenty of exercise. Also, remember the omega 3s; you want to make sure she gets some of those because overweight horses tend to be insulin resistant. You can listen or read my teleseminar, *The Easy Keeper*, for a full explanation about keeping a horse of this type healthy; it's available through my website.

Triple Crown Safe Starch, Dandruff. Debbie has five horses, all with different needs. She uses beet pulp soaked with timothy half a cup of some ration balancer. She was also using alfalfa cubes until one of her older mares choked on them. But then she put the horses on Triple Crown Safe Starch forage with beet pulp and a ration balancer, and everyone seems happy about it. However, her geldings have developed dandruff in their manes. Debbie wonders about that and would also like to know if the Safe Starch is a good idea to feed, especially the ones that have a tendency toward sore feet.

Answer. Safe Starch forage is a wonderful product, with 9% NSC, but it's actually designed to replace hay; it's a chopped forage, as you know, with vitamins and minerals added, so if you're not feeding it exclusively, which most people don't, then you do have to give some ration balancer to it, or add some whole foods, or a mix. The dandruff issue is easy to fix; it's an obvious outcome of not enough omega 3s in the diet. If you give your horses omega 3s, whether it be from flaxseed meal or chia seeds or even flaxseed oil, you will notice that the dandruff goes away.

More on Copra Meal. Heidi would like more information on copra meal. She has a 17-hand warmblood, and she has trouble keeping a top line on him. She wants to stay away from soy.

Answer. The copra meal, as I mentioned earlier, is a good source of protein; it's 20% protein, but it's not a complete or high-quality protein. This is the case with most plant sources of protein, they tend to be incomplete, so to make it complete or high-quality, you need to add some other protein sources. Make sure that your grass hay has an adequate amount of protein and then consider feeding some of the other types of protein we've been discussing to just make everything more complete or as complete as possible. Adding alfalfa would be good.

Growing Vegetables for Horses. Jennifer likes to feed a lot of fruits and herbs and nuts and so she is planting a garden next year; it's horse themed and she wants to know what to grow.

Answer. All of the vegetables we've been discussing are acceptable, so it depends on which of those things will grow in your area—the carrots and beets and their greens, and any of the melons and squashes and so on are wonderful things to offer.

Reading Labels. Jennifer also asks how to read feed labels and avoid products like wheat middlings, soybean hulls, molasses and alfalfa meal.

Answer. Some of those things I don't have a problem with. The wheat middlings are generally not human grade and so there is a possibility they may have some pesticides added to them, depending on how they're made and what the manufacturer insists upon. Soybean hulls are actually a good source of fiber. Unsulphured black strap molasses does contain some minerals but even then, if your horse doesn't need the sugar, I would avoid any kind of molasses. As for the alfalfa meal, alfalfa is a really good source of added amino acids to boost the protein quality.

When reading a feed label, bear this in mind: Feeds come in one of two camps. They're either high in starch and sugar (which means they'll contain cereal grains like oats, corn, and barley, and usually also contain some molasses) or they may be lower in starch (usually containing rice bran and wheat middlings and alfalfa meal and so on). In researching for an article I wrote for the *Horse Journal* (January, 2013) I evaluated a number of feeds. The Prime Glow made by ADM Alliance is not bad; it does have alfalfa meal and rice bran and soybean hulls and ground flaxseed meal. The one that I found that has the lowest amount of NSC is called Carb Safe (Poulin Grain).

These commercially fortified feeds have some drawbacks. For example, the added minerals may not be chelated (thereby reducing bioavailability). They may contain grain byproducts, soy, and other things that I expect this audience would rather avoid. So the goal is to offer your horse basic, wholesome feed ingredients, along with the appropriate supplementation, thereby eliminating the need for commercial feeds.

Ingredients in the Wild. Melya asks for some natural sources of vitamins and minerals and probiotics and omega 3s in the wild. She cites the example of horses eating flowers in the wild, and asks if they ate them because of the nutritious pollen.

Answer. Pollen is nutritious, yes, it's very nutritious, but the flowers themselves also contain vitamins and minerals. There are all kinds of different forages that offer a variety of nutrients and vitamins and minerals—flowers and herbs and bark and leaves and grasses and even weeds. There's not a lot of sodium in fruits and vegetables or in grasses but salt can be obtained from licking rocks or finding mineral deposits on the ground. Probiotics are actually *in* the soil; in fact, horses that eat off the ground usually don't need a probiotic supplement unless they have particular health problems, i.e. trouble keeping weight on, or a compromised immune system issues, or old age, or digestive issues, etc. If they're stalled and they're not able to graze and pick up the microbes that are naturally living in the soil, then they probably do need a probiotic.

Natural Calming Substance. Melya also asked about a natural calming substance. She has a horse that sees other horses only over the paddock fence, and so he gets agitated about being by himself without others in his herd.

Answer. Horses really do need to have physical contact with other horses. Over the fence may not be enough and that may be contributing to the behavior. Nutritionally speaking, magnesium is worth trying. Magnesium affects the nervous system and many horses don't get enough of it, so I would consider natural sources of magnesium such as flowers and rose hips, and pumpkin seeds and squash. Chia seeds also have some, as well. Quiessence is a good supplement with magnesium in it. I offer that on my website.

Cocosoya Oil. Karen comments that she finds coconut oil and cocosoya oil to be economical.

Answer. As I mentioned earlier, cocosoya is coconut and soy. Coconut oil by itself can have some antibacterial and antiviral benefits, but cocosoya oil is an inflammatory oil because of the soybean oil, so I don't recommend it at all. There are other oils that horses like. Rice bran oil is pretty tasty. You might try that one.

Feeding Program for "Rich" Grass. Simrat in the Pacific Northwest has a mare that's had laminitis on and off. She feeds her a low-starch pelleted feed with a sprinkling of whole oats. She also feeds whole flax and a supplement called Equerry's Plus (www.animalhealthsolutionsinc.com). She comments that the grass or hay can be rich in her region and she wonders if she is feeding the right things and if the pasture is a problem.

Answer. I'm not sure what we mean by rich but I assume you mean that it's very green and healthy. Therefore, your horse is likely getting enough vitamins and minerals. Omega 3s are also plentiful in grass, but adding some more from flax is beneficial in regulating insulin levels. Whole flax has to be ground—whole flax is not digested, so to get the nutritional value, you would be better off with ground flaxseed.

Make sure to give magnesium because magnesium is an important component in treating laminitis. The first change I'd actually make in your mare's program would be to eliminate the oats; they are dangerous for a laminitic horse.

I looked up Equerry's Plus. It's a probiotic and digestive enzyme; it also has vitamins and minerals. It has only 25 mg of magnesium; I would add to that, to bring it up to at least 5000 mg or 5 grams per 250 to 500 lbs of body weight.

Supplementing Pasture with Hay. Lauren asks if a horse on pasture 24/7 still or also requires hay.

Answer. No, they usually don't. Of course, it depends on the pasture condition, but if it's a healthy pasture, if it's not overgrazed, if it's not infested with a lot of weeds, and especially if there are a variety of grasses, then, no, there's no need for hay. In fact, compared to living grass, hay is quite inferior. But do consider the variety aspect; if it's improved pasture with only one kind of grass, then you may want to round out the nutrition picture by adding some alfalfa hay or feeding some whole foods added to some type of a carrier.

Rose Hips for Vitamin C. Cindy wonders how much rose hips would you need to feed to equate to the daily recommended level of vitamin C for a senior horse. She also asks what benefits rose hips have on hoof quality.

Answer. One tablespoon of rose hips provides about 200 mg of vitamin C. So let's say you wanted to give your horse 3000 mg of vitamin C. That would be almost a cup of rose hips. And, yes, feeding vitamin C from rose hips is an excellent way to keep the hooves in good shape. Vitamin C is necessary for collagen development; collagen is part of the connective tissue which exists in blood vessels, including the small blood vessels that make up the laminae in the hoof.

Supplementing Weak Pasture. Tina in Pennsylvania has five horses that are out on six acres of pasture 24 hours a day. Because the pasture grass is sparse, they also get a bale of alfalfa-grass mix hay a day (20-25% alfalfa), plus three bales of plain grass hay. They also get Red Cal salt/mineral supplement; it's high in magnesium. She asks what more she should be giving them, and how much chia seed would be helpful. She is considering adding alfalfa pellets.

Answer. In other words, you're relying mainly on hay for your horses' forage needs. Hay is deficient in many of the vitamins, in particular vitamin E, vitamin C, beta carotene which is used to make vitamin A, and vitamin D so I suggest you supplement for these. I like the Glanzen Complete because it's a flaxseed meal base so you wouldn't need the chia seeds. You might also consider High Point (by Horse Tech).

If the pasture recovers seasonally, you may not need a supplement during the warmer growing season; instead, if they have adequate pasture, then you can enjoy giving them some more fruits and vegetables to fill in any gaps that may be in the grass. With hay, you'd have to feed too large an amount of fresh fruits and vegetables to make up for its nutritional deficiencies. But in the summer, you can let them enjoy the grass and just make sure they have salt and water.

About the alfalfa pellets: I would feed approximately 10 pounds total of alfalfa per horse per day. So based on your hay being 20% alfalfa, if they're eating about 20 pounds of hay or so, then they're getting about 4-5 pounds of alfalfa from that, so you could give them five pounds of alfalfa pellets. You can add your supplement (Glanzen Complete, for example) directly to moistened alfalfa pellets. And if you want to boost the protein quality further, get yourself some split peas and add that to the alfalfa mix. If you still want to add chia seeds, feed about half a cup twice a day.

Endophyte Toxins and Sore Feet. Simrat asks whether there is any connection between endophyte toxins and sensitive feet. She recently switched hay to a mix that may include fescue. Her hay analysis revealed it to have 2.1% starch, the ESC is 4.4 and the WSC is 15.5.

Answer. Usually endophyte toxins are an issue with feeding fescue to a pregnant mare; the problem also shows up in unexplained weight loss in all horses. I have not come across research that connects endophytes to foot problems. The problem is more likely coming from your hay. Let's do a calculation: To get the NSC, we add WSC to the starch, so 15.5 + 2.1 over the top in terms of safety. That points to the hay as the culprit. You will either need to soak it or find another grass hay that you can dilute it with.

Conclusion

I hope that this teleseminar has demonstrated to you that (with some exceptions we've noted) many of the foods you eat—fruits and vegetables and nuts and seeds and herbs and different types of teas and more—are just as nutritious for your horses as they are for you. Your horse can enjoy them and benefit from them.

Remember that the horse's digestive system is very sensitive. You need to make changes gradually, starting with small amounts. Allow your horse's digestion to get accustomed to it and then feed the introduced foods on a daily or almost-daily basis so that you remain consistent. You don't want to shock the hindgut with excessive gas production or any destruction of the hindgut bacteria, which can lead to colic and even laminitis.

Do take pleasure in adding these different foods. You'll find that they add nutrients your horse just doesn't get from eating the same thing every single day, and this variety will make your horse blossom.

Appendix A
What It Means to Feed Free Choice

The horse's digestive tract is designed to have forage flowing through it every minute of every day. At night, too!

The intestines are made of muscles and require forage to keep them exercised and conditioned, in order to assure efficient nutrient processing and prevent colic. Furthermore, the horse's stomach continuously secretes acid, even when empty; horses need to chew to produce saliva, a natural antacid. Running out of hay is physically painful and mentally stressful, virtually assuring the formation of an ulcer. But that's not all – the hormonal response created by forage restriction tells the horse to hold on to body fat, creating a weight management nightmare and making it very difficult for the overweight horse to lose weight.

The solution: Feed your horse the way he was designed to eat.

Step 1: *Know what you are feeding.* Test your hay and/or pasture. Especially when feeding overweight horses, the forage should be low in non-structural carbohydrates (NSC)—NSC should be less than 12% on an as-sampled basis. And it should be low in calories (known as digestible energy) at no more than 0.88 Mcals/lb on an as-sampled basis.

Step 2: Once you have determined the forage is appropriate to feed, **feed it free choice**. Always have forage available, 24/7. The hay should never run out, not even for 10 minutes. And not just during the day—nighttime is important, too.

Then be patient, step back and watch your horse do what comes naturally. Give the process approximately 2-3 weeks; most horses take less time, some take up to a month. At first he will overeat, but once he gets the message that the hay is always there, he will walk away – that's the magic moment! He will calm down, eat more slowly, and self-regulate his intake, eating only what his body needs to maintain condition.

Allow your horse to tell you how much he needs. He may even eat less than before because running out of hay is no longer an issue. Trust this will happen. Soon, your horse's weight will adjust into the normal, healthy range, his behavior will be more natural and steady, and his health will be more vibrant.

Appendix B
Antioxidants — The Unsung Heroes

Antioxidant. The word implies that it *goes against* something involving oxygen. But oxygen is necessary for life, so why need something contrary to it? Truth is that oxidation of carbohydrates, proteins, and fats within your horse's cells is an ongoing process and is necessary for the production of energy to fuel work, maintenance, and normal metabolic pathways. As a result of oxidation, free radicals are formed – many thousands of them each day. And they have an important function in destroying bacteria and viruses, serving a role in protecting your horse's immune function. But if the horse is experiencing physical or mental stressors (e.g., strenuous exercise, illness, pain, traveling, stall confinement, etc.), the level of free radical formation can overpower the body's ability to counteract them, leading to the destruction of normal, healthy cells.

A free radical is an unbalanced molecule; it is missing an electron. To ease this "discomfort," the free radical will steal an electron from balanced cells, starting a chain reaction of "electron stealing" from cell to cell, leading to tissue damage, disease, and accelerated aging.

The antioxidant is the hero – it stops this damaging rampage in its tracks by giving of itself – donating its own electron to the free radical. Since the antioxidant is now unstable itself, *it is important to include several antioxidants in the diet to ensure that the unstable one is neutralized and able to function again.*

Made in the USA
Lexington, KY
06 February 2017